I0750302

FINISHING LINE PRESS
www.finishinglinepress.com

Unrequited Love and Other Things of Equal Importance

poems by

Alejandro Ruiz del Sol

Finishing Line Press
Georgetown, Kentucky

Unrequited Love and Other Things of Equal Importance

ISBN 978-1-64662-508-6 First Edition

ACKNOWLEDGMENTS

Barren Magazine first published "w/an Abundance of Caution" in their issue No.5
Okay Donkey first published "Manilla Folder" on August 19, 2019
The Shore Poetry first published "When I Dream of Laundry, This Tether Sways above Me" in The Shore Issue 2—Summer 2019

Publisher: Leah Huete de Maines
Editor: Christen Kincaid
Cover Art: Bonnie Jean Frye
Author Photo: Saúl Ramirez
Cover Design: Elizabeth Maines McCleavy

Printed in the USA on acid-free paper.
Order online: www.finishinglinepress.com
also available on amazon.com

Author inquiries and mail orders:
Finishing Line Press
P. O. Box 1626
Georgetown, Kentucky 40324
U. S. A.

Table of Contents

w/ an abundance of caution 1

Clearwater, Florida (2018) 3

Ya'll 5

Doodlebug 6

Body Speak 8

The Most Beautifulist in the World 10

When I Dream of Laundry, This Tether Sways above Me 11

W-4 13

Email to Therapist 14

A Red Poem (Sailor's Delight) feat. Taylor Swift 15

Excuse me while I disassociate 16

I am your twin, Dada 17

Hold // This Is Rain 18

Manila Folder 19

A Star Is Born! 20

Scam Artist 21

Tomorrow 22

Sweet things to say in bed, alone or otherwise 23

Unrequited Love and Other Things of Equal Importance 24

This book is dedicated to Apollo, Adrianna, and Andrea

"By chance, are you free?"
—Busdriver

w/ an abundance of caution

from my bedroom window I see
        those kids sitting on the edge
of that rusty water tower
looking off into that distance
just swamps and marshes over there

that'd be unique for them
                that vantage point

they're probably seeing the
sun set—their faces
look so golden from down here

that'll make for a good memory, good
for them

someday—
I thought I'd climb that tower, see the land myself,
        yet,
yet the rust and heavy greenery frighten me

and I've been

distracted by low hanging flowers
so abundant you could hide between the petals

So much—I've
                wasted time. Now

I'll
move towards that tower—I'll

burn that damn
tower down. the sun too if I could

dammit

I want no more shame for
that lumpy bed I lay in
the lonely spaces I pace—making good
plans, adventures I won't take.
my own fault / it's my own fault

Then, I'll force my body up at night
the heat makes it easy   and go directly
into those marshes and swamps the
kids were seeing

with hope
for an alligator to
give my body purpose

Clearwater, Florida (2018)

wind chill
air, wet, cold air that's
much worse for

your innards—it chills 'em—

like wieners stored in the freezer.
...

Just wait for the perfume to come

Clearwater is: payday loans
that take months to
repay. Only to do another
for Christmas.

For Christmas! Happens every year
when you're so close to :money: zero. Happens
every year,

like when flowers bloom and produce perfume for
to be sold to you

couldn't consider paying
it back till tax refunds come in.

And to count the petals
of those flowers' bloom'd
would be to count the crop
of lovely days left broken.

Clearwater is: swimming through murky
waters into pastel colored homes
where the wood is soft
and the walls sweat, sweet

smells like perfume
of

whomever just walked past
my miniature cave in this here library

O, whomever you are
if we'd talk

of frozen wieners
and
walls that smell like you.

Ya'll

This next song is for my observer in the back,
their present company excluded,
although, I'm not so sure they have company,
or if the lights in here are so bright, I have misled myself.
And if so perhaps all that is back there is mopheads.

This next song goes out to my observer
I see you in that distance, behind these burning stage lights.

I wrote this musical number that I mean for you
to digest and find ulterior motives behind my lyrical maneuvers.
Although, you may not hear my words exactly.

This next song will be hummed. And otherwise obtuse.
This is my fraudulent exchange. Forgive me.
Could I fool you into believing me?

You, mophead in the back, what does this mean for you?
Here is my next song...

Doodlebug

i.

How long shall I scribble
blue on this black canvas,,
till these lingering
cirrus clouds leave me?

I call this one
"falling in love w/
my best self"

"But it wont
work out. I,
cause mtns. Then,

I crumble. Whom of you learned
that crack pipes crackle? That
there is a resilient stink to it? That you
should avoid happy faces? I,,
create
like this; split lips."

ii.

"Blood in my beard,
matted, my blood.
Why do they attack me?

I am with myself when I scribble
blue rocks on this canvas.
It is such a struggle to be coherent."

iii.

“

attack me

with
rocks
It is such .”

iv.

“Leave those mtns
to form and crumble
on their own. If they
choose to jump off the
Memorial causeway, well that’s
just how some nights end.”

v.

Some ask how I build bridges on rocks.
Ask someone else. I need to finish my paintings.

Body Speak

i.

When in despair
the body is speaking

best advice I can offer is
to find a sky to look up in to
even if it's overcast

forget that though—now
this is what I see

ii.

you let my hairy legs
on your lap, you
don't mind my hairy
body, actually, you
rub my skin like a pet.

iii.

I rest my head
on the arm of the couch.

I take hold of myself and hear

the music
but just beeps tapping my ears drums
& I'd like to stand up to find something
to smoke because I'm *out of breath.*

& I bet this despair will pass
before you have enough of
rubbing my hairy skin
& I bet I can hold my breath

iv.

muffle my body-voice
my uncontrollable tears
let the memory pass
remember,
memories don't reflect today,
I mean typically.
                                        It is so easy for predators
                                        to punch bruises into bruises.

v.

my eyes are away
from the clouds
the moon & the sun
I'm falling into my body—

The Most Beautifulist in the World

Holding hands with
the sun and the sand
as backdrop.

My mind's playing
tricks on me
again, I'm holding
my own hand again.

Laughing at absurd things, twin
mountains with faces that scold us,
say love doesn't work like sand,
doesn't melt into mirrors.

Then the Safety Harbor pier
when at night the water is
calm and reflects the causeway. We
can watch the streetlamps glisten.

Is it only me who imagines
this   as love? I doubt
that but

the thought of how fragile

this is lonely to me. And
is where I find myself.

My hand resting in yours,
your smile is so subdued.

When I Dream of Laundry, This Tether Sways above Me

I'd fold for my tether, I'd
sleep on the wooden floor
below my tether. Use my finger
tips to teach myself routines. I
feel rhythms when
I dream of laundry. When,
when can I feel free? How,
how do I learn to say hello?

again and again.

This is dedicated
to when memories
beget memories. Dedicated
to bedsheets on floors,
a neglected kid who lies
about having bad days.

I'm with you, I'll
climb my tether.

Would it be terrible to hear
how I occupy rooms?
How I pick the green off bread?
Lay on floors just to imagine
a tether swaying above me?
I'd love it if I could
snore slowly. Instead

I wake up to a sea of
backwashed beer cans and
the buzz of streetlamps,
knocking sheets around
wondering how much longer?

Wondering
how much soap? The delicate cycle?
The laundromat? The quarters? The road
I walk to get home?

I'll climb my tether. And,
it might break, and

I'd only know the world
ended if there were no
more sheets to fold.

What are my options then? Paint
model cars? Press
flowers into books?

W-4

Oh, paycheck, my lover,
give me two weeks in peace.

Why am I trouble? Who's the
fucker made me a dog?
How often do they bark? Porch
or patio? Courage smoked or drank?

Maybe this paycheck will last.
Otherwise trouble. Follow

roads of tar or dirt? Lover—
flowers grow here for us.

Chrysanthemums. Blossoms. Orange peels?
Soda cans? A blown tire.
Thoughts of you I plant here. Limited

earning potential, I have.

An empty gas tank. An SUV
that requires guts to drive.

A hammer and WD-40.
Another job to keep things going.

A dog to make a fucker.
Year to another damn year.

Email to Therapist

Thank you, our session
today was helpful!
I had a question,
you know the answer?
Hope
it's okay if I ask?

Assuming insurance
also covers emails? Or
maybe this is a loophole.

I've always been fond
of loopholes, and other
ways of cheating the system.

And speaking of insurance,
what if I didn't have any?
How much might this cost?
What is the cost of an email?

I'm asking for a friend, actually.

I don't
pretend to understand your business,
but maybe you could do
a 2-for-1 special? Cure
two diseases in one session,
or one disease in two?

To me, it sounds like simple economics.

A Red Poem (Sailor's Delight) feat. Taylor Swift

A cloud that looks blue is truly red.
I recognize this in Taylor Swift. In a hallucination
in a meadow in someplace safe.

Like an Insta poem of only emojis.
26 emojis long to describe
each year I ached from money problems
and for this exact kind of thing that I
cannot find the proper name for.

Artists like us make walls this way.
As we build walls and ask our lovers
to reconfigure the walls and notice
that the walls are actually doors. We

hide in caves and light fires all day
and night to represent our significance
to this world and our dominance
over nature. Like ripping petals

from grown up flowers and rubbing our
fingers clean on our Levi's.

Taylor and I walk down paved roads together.
She gazes into her hands to feel her lumpy fingertips.
I look at the pavement, notice a red puddle, and smile. I wave
goodbye to Taylor and her guitar—
for she moves continuously forever.

I kneel over and look inside. The waters
at the Safety Harbor pier have settled,
I see two manatees floating there, eyeing
real estate for when Florida sinks to
the bottom of the ocean.

Excuse me while I disassociate

I want to see a tree   wrapped in a red blanket
and call it myself,   to scratch   my neighbor's
window with my branches   to remind my friends
that some years   have passed   since the last

time I was struck by lightning,

                                        to have
the thought of being cut down   pondered
over me,   my body   sliced and dried.

to be struck   by lightning   a second time
and be entertainment   as
                                        I
                                                turn
                                                        to   snow.

after all, maybe finally   I'll see my life
for what it is.   I hide   in caves and   make
promises   to rocks. I say, "I won't   leave
this cave, or   the alligators that wander about,
I am both herder and   immovable object."

Excuse me while I return from my disassociation.
This is all to digress, to avoid the dying tree.

I am your twin, Dada

With a cupped hand
to give it sound, you

played my skin
like a bongo drum, I

listened to the beat
and ignored the yelling.

Simply, it was a lesson in rhythm—
to be learned quickly.

You placed a cupped hand
on my head when

those men laughed, they were
glad I had skin like them,

not like yours, you
Dada. You stayed calm. I remember.

Your father died, a magician
for dogs, a hero to me, his

grandchild, who whines at grocery stores.
(Thank you, I was doomed without juice.)

Dada told me: *I'm looking at him and he*
looks so much like you.

I whimper with cupped hands, offering
my spit to the sand.

Hold // This is Rain

My Mama told me how much she
kissed the moon. I love to hear her laugh,
there, happy now? This has all been

about her, the introduction is the most
fun thing to read in a book. Because it
sets up the view of the hurricane. I once

had a dream that my Mama came
back from California to show me
how she kisses the moon. As if
it wasn't a metaphor. She kissed it
how you might eat stringed cheese. She laughs

like she loves the sound of farts. A nightmare is like
a pinched nerve or a pulled hair. I'm glad

I never saw her nightmares. I hope
she thinks of cheddar cheese, and I love her.

I was half asleep the morning she left
to be kissed by fresh mozzarella cheese, I don't
remember if we said goodbye though
I remember her silhouette in the doorway, her mission
to feast among mice.

her silhouette in the doorway // the ebb and flow of tides.

Manila Folder

During a
very important business
meeting, I excuse myself

Excuse me   They mock
I say in earnest. I walk
away—take the elevator down,

unbutton my blazer, find my
manila folder I keep hidden
behind the trash receptacle.

It contains the leaves
of my childhood. Buses
and bills. Roads and

nights. Smells of
maple syrup and bread,
chili chicken and Pine-Sol,
clay, gasoline.

I can be a businessman and
keep this here a secret.

A Star Is Born!

A caterpillar on a leaf
                    and bounds.
The leaf

        bends under

            the shock of caterpillar expression.

        Notice that experience.

A cathedral
            of rain.
Jesus
                    would never buy a bike for a caterpillar.
My legs
            wobble from appreciation of the moment.

Later,
        A moth dies in my car's grille.

No more potential.

Scam Artist

Does that palm tree bend further
in the parking lot or here?
I bet it does more up here,
with all this wind.
And what soil does it grow from?
How long did it take? When will it break?

Working at a call center,
I think it's good that I question my surroundings.

And did I forget to tell you I'm on a call?
This fucker can wait, complaining
about nothing, I'm here to feed this
fucker's anger, no resolution required.

And I like the fuckers who scam
the system. I can always tell
when they do. The calculation
in their voices gives it away,
I pretend not to notice.

Or the betting nature of those
whom call me from prison, asking
to be transferred, asking actually
for more time to talk with a
secret someone—I don't question them.

I transfer. Keep my head low. Pretend I'm ignorant.

The abusers. The beggars, The flirts.
The I don't give a fuckers. I hate them
because I'm no different.
                And.
                                And.
                                                And.
This system deserves to be scammed.

Let's sneak it all to our side slowly,
you and me and the group,
and the police won't notice.

Tomorrow

Tomorrow, what will happen
to the doors we opened today?

Tomorrow, I want to eat ice cream
and call it soup.   What else can I do

when my body breaks?

Will you marry my hand?   Cut it
off and drink my blood? I happen
to be a giver. You happen to be a giver.

To give up   my skin to you
when you call me pretty. The words
    we said
that cause us   to close
doors and   wait for tomorrow.

Call
        me pretty.

Tomorrow,   open a window,
breath in   what is there.

This is how we know,
Spring starts today.

Sweet things to say in bed, alone or otherwise

I want to speak to everyone in this bed,
and say,   *I love you grotesquely*
But backtrack
                    and sidetrack what I mean

by love I am like
                    a young dog mistaking
          a shaggy carpet for the wonderful
outdoor grass, although by

this time of year the outdoor grass
is comparable to a tread-bare rug.

The librarian knows I'm an alligator, and now,
this means it's time for bed.
                              I mean to be heard.

I feel a churning in my belly, my veins pop and
throb—of course I feel anxious.

Of course I am thinking.   But not how is wanted.
                         I want my soul to
                         command my body.
I want to be the zoo
                         flamingos thrive in.

I lie as much as I
                    lie under fashionable oak trees, a
protection from
                    the water boiled suns of Florida.
I remember these stories
                         after speaking sweet things
                       in bed,
                        alone or otherwise.

Unrequited Love and Other Things of Equal Importance

(I can remember dinosaurs, like, my grandma.)

Crows with beaks that twist port & starboard. God
is not a utilitarian like how I remembered.

(Who wears eyeglasses?)

One & Two. There's a path through. Three &
Four. Do not lock the door behind you.

Five & Six. Buried in the cellar. Seven &
Eight. Are Nine alligators in vogue.

(And noticed my tapered buttocks and called it significant?)

River &
Maple. They are dogs whom are friends to be

believed. Although they too leave, or,
more likely gallop! I can see River dance for me
like a thrown stone at the edge of a lake,

like a horse in dressage, away and away from me,
I fear. And, I can see

Maple walk parallel to my walk, as a friend might
through meadows packed with dandelions.

(Do you remember how to speak Spanish, too? Likewise.)

In the morning my sea legs tremble.
All because of the drink. Saint
Maria in unrequited love and other things of
equal importance. Teddy Roosevelt and his father's

god damn trees, making a mess for the poor,
deer, and bunnies. Listen, Teddy, who might
you be? Listen to Saint Maria's suggestions
about the process of love, the steps
to resolve a flat tire. She whispers in your ear
as if she were the admirer, like how you might
ride the railing.

(Look at me, I'm great at cleaning, call me a utility.)

Crocodiles speak so eloquently, they're our dinner guests
when God is not watching and the dog is in the kennel.

(The dinosaurs have finally reached me with the leaves and berries
and branches required to end my coiled sleeping patterns.)

(They said leaves and berries and branches taste bitter, and then they walked away. Now expect to see me sleep in parks and under causeways and in unincorporated areas. I sleep as if I were in line at Disneyland. I wait for turkey legs.)

Alejandro Ruiz del Sol is from Florida and California but resides in New Mexico as a recent graduate of New Mexico State University's MFA program. Their work tends to be atmospheric, vocal, and strange. Find more of Alejandro's work online @ GuguTheGadget and www.GuguTheGadget.com

www.ingramcontent.com/pod-product-compliance
Lightning Source LLC
LaVergne TN
LVHW051023080826
845145LV00009B/2773

* 9 7 8 1 6 4 6 6 2 5 0 8 6 *